The Failure of Success

Much has been published about the principles of success. Success and failure, however, may be defined in different ways by different people. Is there an absolute standard for success and failure? Do we win or do we lose when our accomplishments cost more than we can afford?

In the following pages, **Bill Crowder** brings these issues into focus by examining the life of the Old Testament prophet **Jonah**—one man who personally modeled and experienced "the failure of success."

—*Mart DeHaan*
RBC Ministries

This Discovery Series Bible Study is based on
The Failure of Success: The Story of Jonah (Q0720), one of the popular Discovery Series
booklets. Find out more about Discovery Series at
discoveryseries.org

DISCOVERY HOUSE

P U B L I S H E R S®

Managing Editor: Dave Branon
Study Guide questions: Bill Crowder
Graphic Design: Steve Gier

COVER IMAGE: Photos by Rebecca Phillips and Kym Parry (FreeImages.com)

INSIDE PHOTOS:
Courtesy of NASA, p.6; Greyson Ferguson (Freerange Stock), p.8; Julia Freeman-Woolpert (FreeImages.com), p.18; Alex Bruda
(FreeImages.com) and Viktors Kozers (RGBStock), p.20; U.S. National Oceanic and Atmospheric Administration (Public
Domain) and Asif Akbar (FreeImages.com), p.21; Mirko Delcaldo (FreeImages.com), p.28; Caspar Luiken (Public Domain), p.30;
Rupert Jefferies (MorgueFile), p.31; Fredarch (Creative Commons), p.38; PhotoDisc, p.40; Mantasmagorical (MorgueFile.com)
and Photon312 (FreeImages.com), p.41; Piotr Menducki (FreeImages.com), p.48; Ruben G.S. (FreeImages.com), p.50;
Chaleerat Ng (FreeImages.com), p.51; Mihai Tamasila (Stock.XCHNG), p. 54; Joe Rooster (FreeImages.com), p.56

ISBN: 978-1-62707-063-8
Printed in the United States of America
First Printing in 2014

Table of Contents

How To Use

The Purpose

The Discovery Series Bible Study (DSBS) series provides assistance to pastors and lay leaders in guiding and teaching fellow Christians with lessons adapted from RBC Ministries Discovery Series booklets and supplemented with items taken from the pages of *Our Daily Bread.* The DSBS series uses the inductive study method to help Christians understand the Bible more clearly.

The Format

READ: Each DSBS book is divided into a series of lessons. For each lesson, you will read a few pages that will give you insight into one aspect of the overall study. Included in some studies will be FOCAL POINT and TIME OUT FOR THEOLOGY segments to help you think through the material. These can be used as discussion starters for group sessions.

RESPOND: At the end of the reading is a two-page STUDY GUIDE to help participants respond to and reflect on the subject. If you are the leader of a group study, ask each member to preview the STUDY GUIDE before the group gets together. Don't feel that you have to work your way through each question in the STUDY GUIDE; let the interest level of the participants dictate the flow of the discussion. The questions are designed for either group or individual study. Here are the parts of that guide:

MEMORY VERSE: A short Scripture passage that focuses your thinking on the biblical truth at hand and can be used for memorization. You might suggest memorization as a part of each meeting.

WARMING UP: A general interest question that can foster discussion (group) or contemplation (individual).

THINKING THROUGH: Questions that will help a group or a student interact with the reading. These questions help drive home the critical concepts of the book.

DIGGING IN: An inductive study of a related passage of Scripture, reminding the group or the student of the importance of Scripture as the final authority.

GOING FURTHER: A two-part wrap-up of the response: REFER suggests ways to compare the ideas of the lesson with teachings in other parts of the Bible. REFLECT challenges the group or the learner to apply the teaching in real life.

OUR DAILY BREAD: After each STUDY GUIDE session will be an *Our Daily Bread* article that relates to the topic. You can use this for further reflection or for an introduction to a time of prayer.

Go to the Leader's and User's Guide on page 57 for further suggestions about using this Discovery Series Bible Study.

A "Successful" Failure

Apollo 13

The movie *Apollo 13* tells the story of the real-life experience of Jim Lovell and his NASA space crew. The purpose of their mission was to land on and explore the moon, but a life-threatening in-flight explosion crippled the spacecraft. Suddenly, the goal changed. Mission Control in Houston spent the next several days trying to direct the repair of the dying spacecraft and save the lives of the three astronauts aboard. In the end, the mission was seen as a success because the crew returned safely. Yet it was a failure because Apollo 13 never achieved the original goal of landing on the moon. It was a "successful" failure.

The same could be said of the prophet Jonah. The book that bears his name shows that in spite of Jonah's many personal failures, God successfully directed an amazing rescue.

Ironically, the prophecy of Jonah is often seen as a part of the Old Testament that reflects the heart of God for the nations of the world. But Jonah, the man, doesn't deserve the credit. From beginning to end, he was a reluctant participant in God's mission of mercy.

The bigger picture is that Jonah's failure to care about the people of

Nineveh reflected the attitude of his countrymen as well. Together, he and the whole nation of Israel seemed oblivious to the fact that something had gone terribly wrong with the Ninevites and that their lives were hanging in the balance. The fact that these people, who were about to die, were Israel's worst enemies is all part of this amazing story.

Here's Jonah

Jonah 1:1 starts out: "Now the word of the LORD came to Jonah the son of Amittai." *Jonah*, which means "dove" in Hebrew, is identified as the son of *Amittai*, which means "truthful." According to 2 Kings 14:25, Jonah was from Gath Hepher, a village about two miles northeast of Nazareth. Second Kings 14 also helps us to date Jonah's life sometime during Jeroboam's reign from 793 to 753 BC. Some believe that Jonah began to speak on behalf of God about the time the prophet Elisha was concluding his work.

Keys to the Book

Two keys will prove useful in understanding the real issues in this book.

Key No. 1: The book records Jonah's mission to Nineveh, but it is written to Israel, who hated Nineveh. Because God uses Jonah to confront the hatred of Israel, the prophecy of Jonah is as much about racism as it is about missions.

Key No. 2: Jonah is not the principal character of his own book—God is! God has the first word and the last. He orchestrates the entire drama to show His love for Israel's enemies. As amazing events unfold, we must not get caught up in the props and the staging. The Lord Jehovah, not Jonah, is the central character of this story.

It is this focus that can open our understanding to the real message of Jonah—"The Failure of Success."

1

Jonah: Looking Out for No. 1

n the 1960s, the Beatles recorded the old country song "Act Naturally." The title reminds us that there are some things that we don't have to learn how to do—they just come to us naturally.

This is true when we think of our inclination to run from God. It has been said that all of us must learn to obey, but no one needs to be taught to disobey. Playing the role of spiritual fugitive is a natural instinct of fallen human beings.

As we are introduced to the biblical character Jonah, we see him "act naturally" by showing more shortsighted concern for himself than he does for

God or others. He seems more interested in looking out for himself—for No. 1 —than in caring about anyone else. When God asks Jonah to carry a message of warning to another nation, the reluctant prophet runs in the opposite direction. Let's take a closer look at what was happening in Jonah's heart— and in God's.

Desire of God
(1:1–2)

The word of the LORD came to Jonah . . . , saying, "Arise, go to Ninevah, that great city" Jonah 1:1–2.

Nineveh, founded by Nimrod (see Genesis 10:8–12), was on the east bank of the Tigris River, about 550 miles from Samaria, capital of the Northern Kingdom of Israel. (It would take Jonah about a month to walk there at 15 to 20 miles a day.) It was a large city, protected by an outer wall and an inner wall. The inner wall was 50 feet wide and rose 100 feet into the air. This era was the time of Nineveh's greatest glory.

Cry out against it; for their wickedness has come up before Me (1:2).

Notice carefully that Jonah has been asked to carry a message of judgment, not mercy, to this city. God was going to judge the people of Nineveh for their wickedness. He is "Judge of all the earth" (Genesis 18:25). And He must be recognized as such because, even though He is Savior, He is also Sovereign.

God as Judge sent a messenger with a message of judgment, but Jonah declined. Instead of accepting his assignment to speak on behalf of God, the prophet decided to make a run for it.

> Instead of accepting his assignment to speak on behalf of God, the prophet decided to make a run for it.

Desertion of Jonah
(1:3)

WHERE DID JONAH FLEE?

***But Jonah arose to flee to Tarshish from the presence of the LORD** (1:3).*

Jonah's response to God's mission was the opposite of that of Isaiah, who said to the Lord, "Here am I! Send me" (Isaiah 6:8). Jonah was told to arise and go, and he did—but in the opposite direction! He headed for Tarshish, which was 2,500 miles west of Joppa on the west coast of Spain. And Jonah thought he was going to be able to "flee . . . from the presence of the LORD," which was impossible.

Psalm 139 makes it clear that it is impossible to escape the presence of the Lord. Still, Jonah attempted what Adam and Cain had tried before him—to run from God's presence. And he did this rather than to obey the Lord's command.

WHY DID JONAH FLEE?

Jonah understood God's judgment, but he also understood God's mercy. And, as we will see, Jonah did not want Nineveh, the capital of an enemy nation, to be forgiven. Because Jonah knew the willingness of God to forgive sin when there is true change of heart, he fled rather than tell the Ninevites of the coming judgment. He didn't want them to escape God's wrath.

> Jonah fled rather than tell the Ninevites of the coming judgment. He didn't want them to escape God's wrath.

Over the years, some have tried to excuse Jonah's response. Some say the difficulties of the assignment dissuaded him because it would take a month of hard travel to get there, and it would take a three days' journey just to get from one side of the city to the other (3:3).

Others say that Jonah thought the task was too dangerous. The evil of Nineveh was legendary in ancient times, and it was often experienced first-hand by the Jewish people (see Nahum 3:1–5).

Still, at the root of Jonah's unwillingness to go to the citizens of Nineveh was a great hatred for them. They had proven themselves again and again to be the enemies of Israel. They were seen as cruel torturers who descended on rival nations like a plague of locusts—destroying and consuming all.

For Jonah to go to Nineveh would have been the moral equivalent of asking a Jewish resident of New York City in the 1940s to go to Berlin and give the Nazis a chance to be forgiven. The racial tension was so strong that, rather than obey, Jonah fled.

FOCAL POINT

Put yourself in Jonah's shoes. Think about a task you feel God asked you to do in His name: a hard task. How did you feel? Did the idea of fleeing cross your mind?

The prodigal prophet would learn the cost of hatred, and he would learn it the hard way. In his book *Four Minor Prophets,* longtime educator and Bible scholar Frank Gaebelein wrote:

> In a day when prejudice and hatred inflame men's emotions and pervert their judgment, Jonah speaks with compelling force about limiting our love and sympathies only to some of our fellow human beings and excluding others from our pity and compassion (p. 25).

It is easier to hate than to love—and some of us may often find ourselves dangerously close to creating our own Nineveh. Perhaps the people that inhabit our "Nineveh" are abortionists, homosexuals, political enemies, cultists, or an ethnic group we are uncomfortable with. The question we must honestly consider is this: Will our prejudice cause us, like Jonah, to be guilty of silence, or will we intentionally express the heart of our God?

Jonah chose silence and hate rather than obedience and love.

HOW DID JONAH FLEE?

[Jonah] went down to Joppa, and found a ship going to Tarshish; so he paid the fare, and went down into it (1:3).

A boat sailed from Joppa to Tarshish only a few times a year. There was room for him on the ship, so he paid the fare, got on board, and headed west.

At this point, Jonah might have felt affirmed in his actions. Everything was working out, the pieces were falling into place, the circumstances of life were confirming his plan—but the sad reality is that he was still more concerned about himself than others. How easy it is to justify our actions, especially when the wind is at our back. But circumstances, like the wind, can quickly change.

 # Desperation of the Sailors (1:4-5)

GOD'S REACTION (v. 4)

But the Lord sent out a great wind on the sea, and there was a mighty tempest on the sea, so that the ship was about to be broken up.

The phrase "but the Lord" is in direct contrast to "but Jonah" in the preceding verse. The Lord who called Jonah now pursued His wayward servant.

The text says that God "sent out" a great wind, which in the Hebrew is a graphic word for "threw down or flung" (the same expression is used in 1 Samuel 18:11 for Saul throwing down his javelin at David). It is a term that described the wind striking the sea with such great force that it rocked the ship.

The result of God's action was "a mighty tempest on the sea." This phrase brings to mind a contrast. In Mark 4, when Jesus was on the stormy Sea of Galilee, He *calmed* the storm. But here He *caused* it! And it's interesting to note that God's human servants (Jonah in this case) may disobey Him, but His servants in nature (the wind and the sea) always obey Him.

THE SAILORS' RESPONSE (v. 5)

Then the mariners were afraid; and every man cried out to his god, and threw the cargo that was in the ship into the sea, to lighten the load.

Jonah's disobedience caused problems not only for himself but also for those around him. The sailors were innocent bystanders (like the family of Achan in Joshua 7). They were simple, hardworking men who were caught in the middle of Jonah's battle with God.

What was their response? It was threefold:

- *First, they had an emotional response*—they "were afraid." This is notable because these veteran sailors were experienced on the Mediterranean Sea. They knew the nature of the storms there, and they knew that this was no ordinary storm.

- *Second, they had a spiritual response*—"every man cried out to his god." You may criticize these sailors for their "foxhole prayers," but everyone on board was praying—except Jonah! Although he was supposed to be a man of God, Jonah was, practically speaking, acting like the only atheist on board.

> The sailors were innocent bystanders who were caught in the middle of Jonah's battle with God.

- *Third, they had a practical response*—they "threw the cargo . . . into the sea, to lighten the load." They viewed death as being so imminent that their desire for survival outweighed their need for income.

JONAH'S RESPONSE (v. 5)

But Jonah had gone down into the lowest parts of the ship, had lain down, and was fast asleep.

In the midst of the storm, while this flurry of activity was taking place on deck, Jonah was fast asleep! How was this possible? He seemed to be at peace. But we know he was at odds with God. Sometimes we claim that a sense of peace is a good way to measure whether a certain decision is the right one. But maybe this spiritual barometer is really a self-delusion and not the peace of God at all. Commentator Merrill Unger wrote:

> In his backslidden condition [Jonah] was "fast asleep," the result not of submission to God and trust in Him, as in the case of our Lord's sleep on Galilee's stormy lake (Mark 3:37–39), but of spiritual numbness produced by a dull conscience.

The Sailors' Remedy
(1:6–9)

So the captain came to him, and said to him, "What do you mean, sleeper? Arise, call on your God; perhaps your God will consider us, so that we may not perish" (v. 6).

In desperation, the shipmaster woke Jonah and pleaded with him to pray. How ironic that the pagan had to call the man of God to prayer!

After trying everything else, the sailors were left with only one possible answer—the storm was the anger of the gods against someone on board. Notice what they tried to do to remedy the desperate situation they were in:

They said to one another, "Come, let us cast lots, that we may know for whose cause this trouble has come upon us." So they cast lots, and the lot fell on Jonah (v. 7).

In ancient times, people sometimes used colored stones to help discern "the will of the gods." In this case it worked, and the lot fell on Jonah. The same God who controlled the storm also controlled the lot that was cast (Proverbs 16:33).

Then they said to [Jonah], "Please tell us! For whose cause is this trouble upon us? What is your occupation? And where do you come from? What is your country? And of what people are you?" (v. 8).

With machine-gun speed they began to probe Jonah with a series of questions that basically consisted of this thread: Who are you, and why is this happening? Jonah replied:

*I am a Hebrew; and I fear the L*ORD*, the God of heaven, who made the sea and the dry land (v. 9).*

Well, that wasn't entirely true, was it? If Jonah really feared God, he would have been traveling east to Nineveh, not west to Tarshish.

I believe that when Jonah identified his God as the One who "made the sea," he was indicating that his God was the One personally responsible for their predicament—and that He was the only solution for it.

 ## Determination of Jonah
(1:10–14)

*Then the men were exceedingly afraid, and said to him, "Why have you done this?" For the men knew that he fled from the presence of the L*ORD*, because he had told them. Then they they said to him, "What shall we do to you that the sea may be calm for us?"—for the sea was growing more tempestuous (vv. 10–11).*

Verse 10 says that after the sailors learned that Jonah was running from God, they were "exceedingly afraid." Why? Initially they feared only the storm; now they feared the God behind the storm.

The essence of fearing God is to recognize His authority, to respect His authority, and to respond to His authority. The sailors did this, but Jonah didn't! Someone once said that unbelievers never look better than when they are compared to disobedient children of God. Since Jonah wouldn't repent, the sailors asked how they could appease this storm-producing God.

[Jonah] said to them, "Pick me up and throw me into the sea; then

the sea will become calm for you. For I know that this great tempest is because of me" (v. 12).

In essence, Jonah was saying, "I would rather die than obey God and preach repentance to people I hate."

How tragic. Jonah could have said, "I repent and you should too!" or "Turn around and get me to Nineveh," or at the very least, "Give me an oar and let me help row." Instead, he seemed to be saying to God, "I would rather die than go with you to Nineveh."

In contrast to Jonah's unwillingness to be involved in sparing the lives of hundreds of thousands of people in Nineveh, notice how hard these heathen sailors worked to save one man's life. And also notice the

> The essence of fearing God is to recognize His authority, to respect His authority, and to respond to His authority.

respect they had for the Lord in contrast to the disrespect Jonah was showing.

*The men rowed hard to return to land, but they could not, for the sea continued to grow more tempestuous against them. Therefore they cried out to the L*ORD *and said, "We pray, O L*ORD*, please do not let us perish for this man's life, and do not charge us with innocent blood; for You, O L*ORD*, have done as it pleased You" (vv. 13–14).*

 ## Dramatic Ending of the Storm (1:15–16)

*So they picked up Jonah and threw him into the sea, and the sea ceased from its raging. Then the men feared the L*ORD *exceedingly, and offered a sacrifice to the L*ORD *and took vows.*

When the stormy sea suddenly fell calm, the storm in the sailors' hearts grew stronger—now they really feared God! Not only had He caused the storm, but He was also able to turn it off when it suited His purposes.

They offered sacrifices of worship to the true God and made vows of commitment to Him. Meanwhile, Jonah sank like a rock—thinking that he had achieved his goal. He was convinced that he had successfully escaped from the presence of the Lord. But had he?

1 Jonah: Looking Out for No. 1

STUDY GUIDE
read pages 8–17

To understand the destructive nature of spiritual disobedience.

MEMORY VERSE
Galatians 6:7—

"Do not be deceived, God is not mocked; for whatever a man sows, that he will also reap."

Warming Up

How do you define success? What is your definition of failure? What is the basis for those definitions?

Thinking Through

1. Why did Jonah flee to Tarshish? If God's message for Nineveh was one of judgment, why would Jonah not want to be a part of it (see pp. 10–11)?

2. Who was put at risk because of Jonah's choice to disobey (see p. 13)? Describe a time when others were positively or negatively affected by your choices.

3. Beneath his disobedience, what was the root problem in Jonah's heart and life? Why did that problem put him in conflict with God's desires (see pp. 15–16)?

Going Further

Refer

In what ways did God's call to Moses in Exodus 3:9–10 parallel His call to Jonah? In what ways was it different?

1. Page 7 states, "Jonah is not the principal character of his own book—God is!" According to Jonah 1:1–4, how did God orchestrate the entire drama to accomplish His purposes?

¹ Now the word of the Lord came to Jonah the son of Amittai, saying, ² "Arise, go to Nineveh, that great city, and cry out against it; for their wickedness has come up before Me." ³ But Jonah arose to flee to Tarshish from the presence of the Lord. He went down to Joppa, and found a ship going to Tarshish; so he paid the fare, and went down into it, to go with them to Tarshish from the presence of the Lord. ⁴ But the Lord sent out a great wind on the sea, and there was a mighty tempest on the sea, so that the ship was about to be broken up.

2. What was the message that God wanted preached at Nineveh (v. 2)? What was Jonah's response, and why was it foolish (v. 3)?

3. How did Jonah's circumstances seem to affirm his decision (v. 3)? What was God's response to Jonah's rebellion (see v. 4)?

Prayer Time

Use the *Our Daily Bread* article on the next page as a guide for a devotional and meditation time relating to Jonah and success.

Reflect

"The essence of fearing God is to recognize His authority, to respect His authority, and to respond to His authority" (p. 15). Did Jonah do this? The sailors? Do you? How?

God's Will or Yours

Years ago a magazine article commented on the rebellious action of Jonah: "It was not his going to Tarshish that was wrong; but it was going there when the Lord had directed Jonah to go to Nineveh that brought God's judgment upon the wayward prophet. Tarshish may have been a better city than Nineveh, but it was no place for a man commissioned to go elsewhere. The real question is not which is the better of two opportunities before me, but rather where is God directing me? It is like rising up to flee from the presence of the Lord to go somewhere other than the way He indicates."

Dr. A. C. Dixon tells of a lady who had a spoiled son. One day when a wasp flew in the window, the boy, seeing its brilliant colors, began crying for it. At last the mother called to the sitter who was tending the child, "What is that boy crying for? Will you please let him have it?" A few minutes later there was a loud scream. "What's the matter?" the mother exclaimed. "He got what he wanted," was the sitter's calm reply. Sometimes in God's great wisdom He allows us to feel the sting and misery of our selfish, disobedient ways, that we may learn through the pain and humiliation that the Lord knows what is best.

Are you a disobedient Jonah fleeing God's will for your life in order to enjoy the "Tarshish of your own desire"? If so, like the wayward prophet, you will get into a "whale of a lot of trouble."

—*Mart DeHaan*

JONAH 1:3
(NIV)—

Jonah ran away from the Lord. . . . [He] sailed for Tarshish to flee from the Lord.

■ Read today's *Our Daily Bread* at **www.rbc.org/odb**

20

2

A Divine Response to Disobedience

WE NOW LAUNCH INTO the passage that makes the book of Jonah one of the most attacked portions of the Bible. In the 1930s murder trial of Leopold and Leob, their attorney, Clarence Darrow, attacked the credibility of a key witness by saying, "You could more easily believe that Jonah was swallowed by a whale." His strategy backfired, however, because much of the jury said they did believe the story of Jonah and the fish. Darrow's clients were found guilty.

 Preparation
(1:17)

The LORD had prepared a great fish to swallow Jonah. And Jonah was in the belly of the fish three days and three nights.

This is the statement in the story of Jonah that is often ridiculed—but it also calls for our faith in a supernatural God who is unlimited by the natural realm. Let's look at verse 17 more closely.

The Hebrew word for *prepared* includes the idea of "creative activity," implying that this particular fish was especially created by God for this specific event.

The text says that God made "a great fish," not a whale as many believe, though certain whales could swallow a man. (A fully grown adult sperm whale has a mouth 20 feet long, 15 feet high, 9 feet wide, and it can eat an entire giant squid whole.) The text indicates, however, that it was a specially prepared "great fish."

And Jonah wasn't just swallowed by the fish; he remained in its belly for three days and three nights. This is important, because in Matthew 12:40 Jesus not only acknowledged the historical fact of Jonah's being in the fish, but He also went beyond that and showed

> In spite of his rebellion, when Jonah repented, God responded. Jonah said to God, "You heard my voice."

its prophetic significance. He said, "As Jonah was three days and three nights in the belly of the great fish, so will the Son of Man be three days and three nights in the heart of the earth."

"At the time Jonah recognized that he was under the hand of God, he was disobedient, wayward, running—but he was still a child of God."

PAUL VAN GORDER

Prayer
(2:1–9)

Then Jonah prayed to the LORD his God from the fish's belly (v. 1).

Jonah did something in the fish's belly that he refused to do when he was in the boat—he cried out to God. Caves, crosses, and stoning pits may be unusual places from which to pray, but nothing tops this! Imagine what it would have been like to experience the swallowing itself. And what about the conditions within this living grave! But it was there that Jonah lifted up his voice to pray. His prayer has several parts:

HIS PRAYER OF REPENTANCE (v. 2)

I cried out to the LORD because of my affliction, and He answered me. Out of the belly of Sheol I cried, and You heard my voice.

Jonah prayed because of his "affliction" (literally: "binding up"), which seems appropriate for a man inside a fish. Notice that the place of his prayers is "out of the belly of Sheol," not just out of the belly of a fish.

What is Sheol? It is pictured in Scripture as being beneath the ground (Job 17:16), a place of darkness (Job 10:19–22), and a place of silence (Psalm 6:5). Although being in Sheol implies separation from God, it is accessible to God. In most cases, Sheol is the realm of the dead. Whether used to speak of the grave or of the realm of existence after death, it is clear that Sheol is a place of death, not life.

Jonah had set out for Tarshish in defiance of God, but he ended up in Sheol. Yet in spite of his rebellion, when Jonah repented, God responded. Jonah said to God, "You heard my voice."

HIS PRAYER OF SUBMISSION (vv. 3–4)

You cast me into the deep, into the heart of the seas, and the floods surrounded me; all Your billows and Your waves passed over me. Then I said, "I have been cast out of Your sight; yet I will look again toward Your holy temple."

Here Jonah comes to his senses. Finally, in the belly of a great fish, he saw the sovereignty of God in spite of his physical circumstances. In the grip of death, he saw God's hand behind all that had happened to him ("*You* cast me," "*Your* billows," "*Your* waves," "*Your* sight"). God was the one who caused the storm to erupt, and He was the one who used the sailors to execute His judgment by casting Jonah into the sea.

Evidence of God's powerful presence in life's circumstances can be seen throughout Scripture. Paul, for example, saw himself as a prisoner of Christ (not Rome). Joseph saw God's hand behind his slavery. Job saw the work of God in his trials. And the Son of God recognized the Father's hand in His suffering.

Besides acknowledging God's power and authority in his circumstances, Jonah also appealed to God's mercy. With hope of being restored to worship, he prayed in verse 4, "I will look again toward Your holy temple."

HIS PRAYER IN TROUBLE (vv. 5–6)

The waters surrounded me, even to my soul; the deep closed around me; weeds were wrapped around my head. I went down to the moorings of the mountains; the earth with its bars closed behind me forever; yet You have brought up my life from the pit, O Lord, my God.

These verses describe the terrifying depths to which Jonah had sunk. His flight from God, a violent storm, deep water, and the hungry mouth of a

"The miracle of Jonah consists in the fact that God raised him from the dead as a perfect type of the gospel of our crucified, buried, and risen Lord."

DR. M. R. DEHAAN

---

monster fish brought him to the threshold of Sheol, the land of the dead ("the earth with its bars closed behind me forever").

Yet, even though Jonah believed that death had claimed him, this part of his prayer ended with hope when he said, "You have brought up my life from the pit." He acknowledged God's loving correction as necessary for his restoration, not his destruction.

HIS PRAYER OF RESTORATION (v. 7)

When my soul fainted within me, I remembered the LORD; and my prayer went up to You, into Your holy temple.

As Jonah was beginning to fade, he prayed for restoration.

HIS PRAYER OF CONFESSION (v. 8)

Those who regard worthless idols forsake their own Mercy.

The New International Version (1984) translates this verse: "Those who cling to worthless idols forfeit the grace that could be theirs." Jonah was confessing his sin of trusting in an idol that could do nothing to save or rescue him, which was a complete waste of time and energy. And what was Jonah's idol? It was self-will—the ultimate idol.

Bowing at the idol of his own will, Jonah had committed himself to

> Jonah was ready to stop worshiping himself at the altar of his own will.

a path of rebellion—the ultimate spiritual failure. Only when he turned to God in repentance would he discover what spiritual success was truly all about.

HIS PRAYER OF THANKSGIVING (v. 9)

But I will sacrifice to You with the voice of thanksgiving; I will pay what I have vowed. Salvation is of the LORD.

This prayer meant two things. He was ready to stop worshiping himself at the altar of his own will. And he was ready to make the turn. Like a broken fugitive with nowhere to hide, he gave himself up. So he declared, "I will sacrifice" and "I will pay what I have vowed." With these words he declared his long-overdue surrender and said, in effect, "Lord, take me to Nineveh."

 ## Power
(2:10)

So the LORD spoke to the fish, and it vomited Jonah onto dry land.

Again, we see the control of God. The winds obeyed. The seas obeyed. Now the fish obeys. The only one who disobeyed was Jonah, the man of God. The sailors couldn't get Jonah to shore, but God used the fish to get him there rather easily.

Jonah's return to dry land was unceremonial and unconventional. The fish vomited him up. This is not a pleasant thought, but it is the only "positive" use of the word *vomit* in the Bible. Elsewhere, *vomit* is used of Israel (Leviticus 18), the rich (Job 20), Laodicea (Revelation 3), a dog and a fool (Proverbs 26:11), and mostly of drunks.

> The winds obeyed. The seas obeyed. Now the fish obeys. The only one who disobeyed was Jonah, the man of God.

Jonah's story began with his "succeeding at failure" as he rejected God's call, disobeyed God's command, and ignored God's will. He worshiped at the idol of self, choosing to die rather than to submit to God. But in grace and in correction, God pursued His wayward servant. Now Jonah, who succeeded so well at spiritual failure, will be given a second chance, another opportunity to get it right.

A Divine Response to Disobedience

STUDY GUIDE 2
read pages 21–27

To see God's power displayed in both discipline and rescue.

MEMORY VERSE
Matthew 12:40—

"For as Jonah was three days and three nights in the belly of the great fish, so will the Son of Man be three days and three nights in the heart of the earth."

Warming Up

Have you had times when your disobedience brought serious consequences into your life? If so, what kind of consequences did you experience?

Thinking Through

1. What was life like in Jonah's new environment (see p. 23)? What elements of that new environment might have caused Jonah to compare it to Sheol?

2. In what ways does Jonah's experience in the great fish call for our faith in a supernatural God? How does it confirm God to be unhindered by the natural realm (see p. 22)?

3. Although our experience is not the same as Jonah's, our need for spiritual correction could be. What parts of Jonah's prayer form a meaningful response to God's correction (see pp. 23–26)?

Going Further

Refer

In Jonah 2:8, Jonah confessed that he had trusted in an idol that could do nothing to save or rescue him. What was that idol? What idols have we trusted in our lives?

1. Having refused to pray in the boat, what did Jonah experience that prompted him to pray? How did he describe his situation? Do you agree with his assessment of the conditions he was in?

2. How did Jonah describe God's activity in confronting him about his refusal to go to Nineveh? How did Jonah see God's hand behind everything at work in his situation?

3. What portion of the Jonah 2:1–4 shows Jonah's hope? Why does it reflect a hopeful perspective?

¹ Then Jonah prayed to the LORD his God from the fish's belly. ² And he said:

"I cried out to the LORD because of my affliction,
And He answered me.

"Out of the belly of Sheol I cried,
And You heard my voice.

³ For You cast me into the deep,
Into the heart of the seas,
And the floods surrounded me;
All Your billows and Your waves passed over me.

⁴ Then I said, 'I have been cast out of Your sight;
Yet I will look again toward Your holy temple.'"

Prayer Time

Use the *Our Daily Bread* article on the next page as a guide for a devotional and meditation time relating to Jonah and success.

Reflect

Jonah's prayer ends in verse 9 with thanksgiving. Have you thanked God recently? If not, why not?

Write a prayer of thanksgiving to God for His blessings in the past week. Now add some from the past month and the past year. Now add some blessings from previous years. Notice how your perspective changes when you count your blessings.

Inside Jonah Inside the Fish

Most people who read Jonah are so taken up with the fish that they pay little attention to the prophet's prayer. Biblical critics, for example, insist that some whales have such small throats they can't swallow anything bigger than an orange. Some believers counter by saying that adult sperm whales have a mouth 20 feet long, 15 feet wide, and 9 feet high, and that they sometimes swallow large animals. They try to add credibility by relating stories —like that of a sailor named James Bartley who was found alive inside the stomach of a harpooned whale the day after he had been ingested.

Although I can't vouch for that story, I'm not much concerned. A miracle doesn't need scientific proof to be believed. Besides, I agree with the scholar who said we must avoid becoming so obsessed with what was *going on inside the fish that we miss the drama going on inside Jonah.* The great miracle was the change in the prophet as he prayed from within the stomach of the sea creature. In recounting his feelings just before he sank into the deep, he told how he had called out to God. Then he felt himself losing consciousness, only to awaken inside the fish. Knowing that this had to be God's doing, he was confident he would be returned to land. And he was ready to do the Lord's will.

God still chastens us when we disobey. He desires that we experience an inward change just as Jonah did inside himself inside the fish.

—*Herb Vander Lugt*

Jonah 2:9—
I will pay what I have vowed. Salvation is of the LORD.

■ Read today's
Our Daily Bread at
www.rbc.org/odb

3

Winning the Battle...

n 1836, a war was waged for the independence of Texas. The leader of Mexico, Santa Anna, was not about to give in to the "Texicans," who were ready to die for their freedom. In March of that year, Santa Anna's soldiers pressed their siege for San Antonio de Bejar for thirteen crucial days. Although they eventually succeeded in storming the Alamo and overwhelming the badly outnumbered Texans, Santa Anna paid a huge price for his victory. While Mexican forces were tied up in the battle for the Alamo, General Sam Houston used the time to organize an army that would defeat Mexico at San Jacinto and allow Texas to become a republic. Santa Anna won the battle, but he lost the war.

As we come to the third chapter of Jonah, the Lord of Israel has won the battle. But as we will see, the war is not yet over.

Back on land, Jonah begins to make his way to Nineveh. He had taken a detour through the belly of a fish, but now he's back on track. In the last two chapters, God will use him to bring about one of the greatest rescues in history. But how will Jonah respond?

 A Second Chance
(3:1–2)

Now the word of the Lord came to Jonah the second time, saying, "Arise, go to Nineveh, that great city, and preach to it the message that I tell you."

Against the backdrop of Jonah's resistance and subsequent remorse, God, in grace and mercy, gave Jonah a second chance to carry out his mission.

Notice that Jonah's second call was much more personal and intense than the first. The first call was general ("cry out against"), but the second call was more specific ("preach . . . the message that I tell you").

A second chance for service is not unheard of. It was given to Moses (Acts 7:25) and also to Peter (John 21). But we must not presume. The Scriptures show that it can be danger-

> The Scriptures show that it can be dangerous to presume we'll be given a second chance.

ous to presume we'll be given a second chance (1 Kings 13:26). A "second call" is never guaranteed. It is much safer to respond favorably to God the first time. In Jonah's case, God could have called a second man, but for His own purposes He chose to call the same man a second time.

A Simple Message
(3:3–4)

So Jonah arose and went to Nineveh, according to the word of the **Lord**. *Now Nineveh was an exceedingly great city, a three-day journey in extent. And Jonah began to enter the city on the first day's walk. Then he cried out and said, "Yet forty days, and Nineveh shall be overthrown."*

Nineveh was great in size, significance, and wealth. But it was also great in its sin (1:2). That is why Jonah was there, and he began a three-day journey through town to declare God's warning to the people.

How did he get a crowd? Bible commentator Harry Rimmer suggests that the fish's gastric juices may have had a dramatic effect on Jonah's appearance by removing his hair and bleaching his skin. The sight of him (and possibly the smell) certainly would have caused people to notice.

> The sight of Jonah certainly would have caused people to notice.

GOD'S JUDGMENT

"Nineveh shall be overthrown!" The word *overthrown* means "to overturn," and the tense of the verb describes it being done with thoroughness—a complete destruction of the city to its foundation. This same word is used in Genesis 19:25 to describe the destruction of Sodom and Gomorrah.

Undoubtedly, Jonah preached more than these specific words, but this was his main theme. As warnings go, his message was short and to the point. Messages of judgment are often marked by such directness:

- Nathan said to David, "You are the man!" (2 Samuel 12:7).
- A message of judgment on King Belshazzar supernaturally appeared on

a wall with the following message: "Mene, mene, tekel, upharsin" (Daniel 5:25).

- The Lord said to the Ephesian church, "Repent and do the first works" (Revelation 2:5).

It's possible that Jonah might have enjoyed his message of judgment a bit too much. He had already shown his hatred for the Ninevites, and now he was pronouncing their coming destruction. He could have easily felt a sense of satisfaction as he preached those words. But if he did find such pleasure, he missed the mercy of God in the message and urgent warning he proclaimed.

GOD'S MERCY

"Yet forty days . . . ." This is the key, for it speaks of God's mercy. If there had been no opportunity for repentance, no deadline would have been needed. But God gave Nineveh a specific amount of time to repent. And what would bring about their repentance? As always, it was the word of God given to people who needed His mercy and forgiveness more than anything else in life.

The irony of Judah's story, however, is that the people of Nineveh were about to honor God with a surrender that Jonah was still not ready to give. Behind and underneath his external obedience, his internal rebellion remained. He had actively rebelled when he fled to Tarshish, but now he was passively rebelling against the heart of God. As we are about to see, even though he was speaking the words of God, he remained out of step with the heart of the merciful God who is "not willing that any should perish but that all [even Nineveh] should come to repentance" (2 Peter 3:9).

A Serious Response
(3:5–9)

What would it have been like to be in Nineveh when Jonah delivered his message? Pastor and author James Montgomery Boice described it like this:

> We can almost see Jonah as he entered a day's journey and began to cry out his message. What would be his reception? Would the Ninevites laugh?

Would they turn against Jonah and persecute him? As he cried out, people stopped to listen. The hum of commerce died down, and a holy hush stole over the collecting multitudes. Soon there was weeping—along with other signs of genuine repentance of sin. At last the message of Jonah entered even the palace, and the king, divesting himself of his magnificent robes, took the place of a mourner alongside his repenting subjects (*Can You Run Away From God?*, pp. 71–72).

What an amazing scene! Notice how an entire culture responded to the grace and mercy of God:

THEIR BELIEF (v. 5)

So the people of Nineveh believed God . . . .

The word *believed* here is identical to the word in Genesis 15:6. "[Abraham] believed in the LORD, and He accounted it to him for righteousness." This isn't just believing what is said; it is trusting God, who has spoken. The people believed that Jonah's message was from God, and they took it seriously. Hebrews 11:6 says that "without faith it is impossible to please [God]." They believed God—and responded!

THEIR REPENTANCE AND PRAYER (vv. 5–9)

So the people of Nineveh . . . proclaimed a fast, and put on sackcloth, from the greatest to the least of them. Then word came to the king of Nineveh; and he arose from his throne and laid aside his robe, covered himself with sackcloth and sat in ashes. And he caused it to be proclaimed and published throughout Nineveh by the decree of the king and his nobles, saying, "Let neither man nor beast, herd nor flock, taste anything; do not let them eat, or drink water. But let man and beast be covered with sackcloth, and cry mightily to God; yes, let every one turn from his evil way and from the violence that is in his hands. Who can tell if God will turn and relent, and turn away from His fierce anger, so that we may not perish?"

Two Old Testament expressions of sincere change of heart are *fasting* and *wearing sackcloth*. Notice that the people's faith produced action—spontaneous, immediate, and unanimous.

Putting on sackcloth (coarse cloth) was a symbol of humiliation, distress, and mourning. It was a declaration of personal unworthiness, and it was done by *all* the people, from the greatest to the least. Even the animals were involved.

The people's repentant faith caused a change in their behavior. No vague or superficial confession would do. A true change of minds and hearts evidenced by changed lives was desperately needed.

In response to Jonah's warning from God, a pagan king led his people in national repentance, acknowledging that God is sovereign and could "turn away from His fierce anger" (v. 9) if He chose to. But the king still called on the citizens of Nineveh to pray for God's mercy. His request expressed faith and hope on the part of the king. It is important to notice that neither the king nor the people of Nineveh had any evidence on which to base their hope except that God had given them a warning instead of immediately destroying them. So, by faith, they went to prayer with hope that mercy would overtake judgment.

 A Saving God
(3:10)

Then God saw their works, that they turned from their evil way; and God relented from the disaster that He had said He would bring upon them, and He did not do it.

WHAT GOD SAW

He saw their works and that they genuinely turned from their sin. The genuineness of their repentance was seen in the evidence of their changed lives (see Luke 3:8; Acts 26:20).

WHAT GOD DID

"God relented . . . and He did not do it." God reversed His declaration of judgment and rescued them from their sin and guilt. This doesn't mean, however, that God repented or changed His mind. Instead, He remained true to His eternal principles of justice and mercy. Consider the following:

- *"The Glory of Israel does not lie or change his mind; for he is not a human being, that he should change his mind"* (1 Samuel 15:29 NIV).

- *"God is not a man, that He should lie, nor a son of man, that He should repent. Has He said, and will He not do? Or has He spoken, and will He not make it good?"* (Numbers 23:19).

The character of God does not change. Instead, as people change in their relationship to Him, different laws come into operation. When verse 10 says that "God relented," it's not referring to His remorse over an error in judgment but a removal of judgment as an act of mercy to one who has repented.

God's laws about judgment of sin are clear, but escape is available when we appeal to Him on His terms seeking mercy and forgiveness. That is how the battle for the hearts of Nineveh had been won.

3

Winning the Battle...

STUDY GUIDE
read pages 31–37

MEMORY VERSE
Numbers 23:19—
"God is not a man, that He should lie, nor a son of man, that He should repent. Has He said, and will He not do? Or has He spoken, and will He not make it good?"

To see the power of God to change repentant lives.

Warming Up

Have you known, lived with, or worked with people who ever changed their mind about something they said they would do? Was it for better or worse? How did you feel about their change of mind?

Thinking Through

1. In Jonah 3:1–4, God gave Jonah a second call to carry out His mission. How were the two calls similar? How were they different? Why should we not presume we will receive a second call (see p. 32)?

2. What was Jonah's specific message? Does his message still apply today? In Nineveh, what kinds of action prompted God's mercy instead of His judgment (see pp. 35–36)?

3. How can you reconcile God's actions in Nineveh with Numbers 23:19 (see p. 37)?

Going Further

Refer

Read 2 Corinthians 7:10. What is the difference between godly sorrow and the sorrow of the world? What kind of sorrow have you experienced most recently? With what effect?

1. In what ways did the king of Nineveh take a primary role in demonstrating national repentance? How did that example impact the people?

5 So the people of Nineveh believed God, proclaimed a fast, and put on sackcloth, from the greatest to the least of them. 6 Then word came to the king of Nineveh; and he arose from his throne and laid aside his robe, covered himself with sackcloth and sat in ashes. 7 And he caused it to be proclaimed and published throughout Nineveh by the decree of the king and his nobles, saying, Let neither man nor beast, herd nor flock, taste anything; do not let them eat, or drink water. 8 But let man and beast be covered with sackcloth, and cry mightily to God; yes, let every one turn from his evil way and from the violence that is in his hands. 9 Who can tell if God will turn and relent, and turn away from His fierce anger, so that we may not perish?

2. What did the king hope would be God's response to the city's repentance? Why do you think the king had such a profound fear of God?

3. Why do you think it was important to the king that even the livestock be involved in the display of repentance?

Prayer Time
Use the *Our Daily Bread* article on the next page as a guide for a devotional and meditation time relating to Jonah and success.

Reflect

God's response changed when people had a true change of heart and mind. What experiences in your own life have prompted/should prompt repentant faith with hope in God's mercy?

Because God is a God of grace, mercy, and compassion, we should also pray for others to turn to Him. End this lesson by praying for your home, your church, your community, your country.

A Second Chance

I know a man who promised the Lord he'd be a missionary but didn't carry out his pledge. Instead he went into the business world and made a lot of money. In his retirement years, however, he did serve in missions. He felt fulfilled and praised God for a second chance.

Jonah is another example of one who received a second opportunity. God went to great lengths to make him willing to preach to the Ninevites. Bible people Jacob, Moses, David, and Peter were also given a second chance. Therefore, if you have made a mess of your life through disobedience, don't despair. When you confess your sin, God will restore you to fellowship with himself and fill you with spiritual joy. He may even give you an opportunity to make up for your failure.

This is an encouraging truth, but it should never cause a believer to think that if he repents quickly he can do anything he wants without paying a price. A man who divorced his wife a few years ago to marry a younger woman has discovered that he didn't sin cheaply. Today he lives with a deep feeling of remorse and is uncomfortable whenever he's around his children and former friends. And though he knows God has forgiven him, he realizes he can never fully undo the wrong.

The teaching about a second chance should encourage us. But it must never be seen as a sanction for disobedience.

—*Herb Vander Lugt*

JONAH 3:1—
Now the word of the LORD came to Jonah the second time.

■ Read today's *Our Daily Bread* at **www.rbc.org/odb**

40

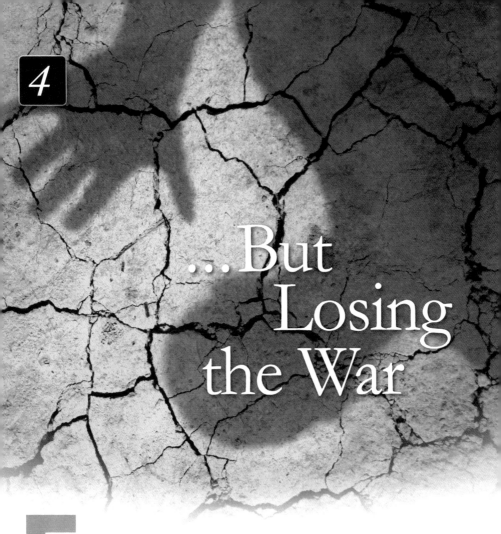

4

...But Losing the War

From our point of view, the story of Jonah could have ended in Chapter 3. The job had been done. Nineveh had repented, and all was well with the world. But Chapter 4 is there for a reason. As we come to the final chapter of Jonah's record, we see him failing at success. After being God's instrument to produce the greatest revival in human history, Jonah was more than upset—he was seething with an anger that wouldn't go away. He had won a major battle, but he was about to lose the war.

It's fascinating to see how quickly Nineveh responded to the work of God, yet how slow Jonah was to respond to the Lord. The abundant mercy that God had on the Ninevites created an overwhelming depth of anger and bitterness in the reluctant prophet.

 Jonah's Anger (4:1–3)

"It displeased Jonah exceedingly...." The word *displeased* means "to see as evil." Jonah actually viewed God's rescue of Nineveh as wrong!

"...and he became angry." The word for *anger* means "to burn." God had mercifully turned from His anger, but Jonah's anger toward God was kindled.

Why was he angry? Because judgment had been averted, and it was a judgment Jonah desperately wanted to see happen! Jonah had done what God wanted him to do—to go and preach—but God had not done what Jonah wanted—to destroy Nineveh. Jonah was angry at God for showing mercy, and he felt betrayed that He had spared the hated Ninevites.

"He prayed...and said..." The last time Jonah prayed, he was in the belly of a fish and glad for mercy. But now he was angry at God for that same mercy. Why? Because it had gone to his enemies.

"...was not this what I said....?" He basically said to God, "I told you so! I was right, and You were wrong." He even tried to justify his rebellion by admitting that his initial act of disobedience was an attempt to interfere with or thwart the mercy of God.

In effect, Jonah was saying, "This is the reason I refused to go to Nineveh when You first called me. And I was right for doing so!" Isn't that what we sometimes do? James Montgomery Boice wrote:

> After being God's instrument to produce the greatest revival in human history, Jonah was more than upset. He was seething with anger.

Things do not turn out as we wish, so we seek to justify our disobedience before God. What we need to learn is that we are not sufficient to pass on the appropriateness or inappropriateness of the outcome, nor are we responsible for it. We are responsible only for performing the whole will of God (*Can You Run Away From God?* pp. 84–85).

"…I know that You are…." Amazingly, Jonah based his argument on the list of divine attributes found in Exodus 34:6–7, God's revelation of himself following the sin of Israel with the golden calf at Sinai. Jonah resented the fact that God is the following:

- "Gracious"—showing favor to those who don't deserve it (like Jonah, who accepted it in 2:9).
- "Merciful"—showing kindness, compassion, and forgiveness to those in need. Jonah had received it, but he refused to extend it.
- "Slow to anger"—God does not always immediately execute the punishment deserved but gives time to repent.
- "Abundant in lovingkindness"—abounding in love, goodness, and pity.
- "One who relents from doing harm"—capable of judgment as well as forgiveness.

Jonah used God's own description of himself in Exodus 34 to accuse Him of being two-faced and inconsistent. Jonah basically said, "I know what You're like. So why did You send me with a message of judgment if You were just going to show them mercy anyway?"

Jonah was so bitter and angry at God that he just wanted to die.

"…take my life from me…." It's amazing that earlier Jonah praised God three times for saving his life (2:5–7). But here, in the first of two times (see also v. 8), he asked God to kill him. Why? Jonah refused to accept God's will because of his own hatred for the Ninevites. His own self-will gripped his thinking so powerfully (using the words *I, me,* and *my* eight times in these two verses) that Jonah would rather die than have them live. What a contrast to the Savior, who gladly died so we could live.

God's Challenge
(4:4)

The Lord said, "Is it right for you to be angry?"

God would not leave this matter unresolved, so He challenged Jonah about his anger. It's not uncommon in the Bible for God to challenge His people with penetrating questions:

- He asked Adam, "Where are you?" (Genesis 3:9).
- He asked Cain, "Where is Abel your brother?" (Genesis 4:9).
- Jesus asked Judas, "Are you betraying the Son of Man with a kiss?" (Luke 22:48).

It's as if God were saying to Jonah, "We are looking at the identical situation in two different ways. Which of us has the proper perspective?" Jonah's answer should have been, "Let God be true but every man a liar" (Romans 3:4). But instead, he ran away again.

Jonah's Flight
(4:5)

So Jonah went out of the city and sat on the east side of the city. There he made himself a shelter and sat under it in the shade, till he might see what would become of the city.

Jonah was concerned only for his comfort—making a shelter where he could sit and watch the city. His festering selfishness had made him into an isolated and bitter man—and without a change of heart a bitter person only gets worse with time. God would deal with His wayward prophet by asking him another question. But first He would take steps to prepare Jonah's heart for the message in that question.

God's Preparation
(4:6–8)

The Lord God prepared a plant and made it come up over Jonah,

that it might be shade for his head to deliver him from his misery. So Jonah was very grateful for the plant (v. 6).

The plant was a rapidly growing plant with broad leaves. Some have identified it as the castor oil plant, which grows about twelve feet high and has large leaves. Notice that for the first time in the entire story, Jonah is "grateful." But it is only because he is benefiting from the plant.

But as morning dawned the next day God prepared a worm, and it so damaged the plant that it withered (v. 7).

The worm had a voracious appetite ("chewed the vine" NIV). Verses 6 and 7 expose two opposite characteristics of God's nature—His ability to deliver and to destroy. The purpose of the worm was to destroy the plant so Jonah would once again be exposed.

It happened, when the sun arose, that God prepared a vehement east wind (v. 8).

The wind was a hot, scorching east wind (often called "sirocco") that blew off the Arabian desert. God responded to the heat of Jonah's anger by exposing him to the heat of the desert and all its elements.

…and the sun beat on Jonah's head, so that he grew faint. Then he wished death for himself, and said, "It is better for me to die than to live" (v. 8).

God supernaturally removed all of Jonah's avenues of retreat so He would have Jonah's undivided attention. But tragically, Jonah still saw death as preferable to submitting to God.

 # God's Question (4:9)

God said to Jonah, "Is it right for you to be angry about the plant?"

In verse 4, Jonah was angry about God. Now he's angry about a plant. Bitterness often begins lofty and ends puny. James Montgomery Boice wrote,

The same thing happens when we become angry. We begin by being angry at big things, but very quickly we become angry at petty things. First we get angry at God. Next we express our anger at circumstances, then minor circumstances. Finally, our shoelace breaks one morning, and we find ourselves swearing. God was showing him this, saying in effect, "Look where your anger has taken you, Jonah. Is this right? Is this the way to live? Do you want to spend the rest of your life swearing at petty annoyances?" (*Can You Run Away From God?* p. 95).

 ## Jonah's Sulking
(4:9)

[Jonah] said, "It is right for me to be angry, even to death!"

Jonah still didn't get it. There he sat, under a withered stalk, despondent, bitter, vindictive—a tragic portrait in self-pity. He was still defending himself and despairing of life. He saw no rationale for God's actions with Nineveh or with the plant, so he decided that if God was going to act this way, he would be better off dead.

 ## God's Rebuke
(4:10-11)

COMPASSION FOR A PLANT? (v. 10)

But the LORD said, "You have had pity on the plant for which you have not labored, nor made it grow, which came up in a night and perished in a night."

God put Jonah's attitude into perspective:
• He loved a worthless plant, but he hated the eternal souls of men.
• He showed compassion for one small element of God's creation but had no mercy for an entire city facing eternal judgment.

COMPASSION FOR A CITY! (v. 11)

Should I not pity Nineveh, that great city, in which are more than one

hundred and twenty thousand persons who cannot discern between their right hand and their left—and much livestock?

Jonah needed to see that compassion for a plant was without value, but compassion for a city with more than 120,000 residents has eternal value. If they couldn't discern right from left, how could they know right from wrong? If Jonah could not pity the people of the city, surely he could pity the cattle—who at least should be as innocent as the plant!

In the midst of this great spiritual awakening, Jonah was still missing the greatness of God's grace and mercy. Having won the battle of reaching Nineveh with God's message, Jonah had lost the war in his own heart.

4 ...But Losing the War

STUDY GUIDE
read pages 41–47

To see the mercy and grace of God on display.

MEMORY VERSE
Exodus 34:6—

"And the LORD passed before him and proclaimed, 'The LORD, the Lord God, merciful and gracious, longsuffering, and abounding in goodness and truth.' "

Warming Up

Jonah became angry when God's plan didn't match his own plan for Nineveh. How do you respond when God's plan doesn't seem to match your own plans?

Thinking Through

1. Why was Jonah so angry with God for showing mercy to the Ninevites (see pp. 42–43)? Have you ever felt disappointed in how God seemed to be handling your life?

2. James Montgomery Boice wrote that we sometimes seek to justify our disobedience when things don't turn out as we wish (see. p. 42–43). Have you ever experienced that? Describe the situation. What were the results?

3. What three things did God send to provide object lessons to Jonah? How is each one significant to his learning process (see p. 45)?

Going Further

Refer

Notice how Jonah 3:10 describes God's response to Nineveh's repentance. What were the elements of that response? Do you believe God still acts the same way? Why or why not?

1. In Jonah 4:7, God prepared a worm to destroy the plant He had created. Jonah became angry at the plant. How did he justify that anger to God?

2. Jonah struggled to see the importance of the eternal over the temporal (vv. 10–11). How is that seen in his life, and how is it seen in ours?

3. God's final words to Jonah (v. 11) challenge the prophet's attitude toward the Ninevite people. How can our anger toward people cause us to be irrational in our reactions to them?

⁹ Then God said to Jonah, "Is it right for you to be angry about the plant?" And he said, "It is right for me to be angry, even to death!"
¹⁰ But the Lord said, "You have had pity on the plant for which you have not labored, nor made it grow, which came up in a night and perished in a night. ¹¹ And should I not pity Nineveh, that great city, in which are more than one hundred and twenty thousand persons who cannot discern between their right hand and their left—and much livestock?"

Prayer Time ➤

Use the *Our Daily Bread* article on the next page as a guide for a devotional and meditation time relating to Jonah and success.

Reflect

Have you ever been involved in God's work of bringing forgiveness to someone? How did you feel about being used of God in this way? Why?

Consider 2 Peter 3:9. What are God's great concerns for people? How or why do we often overlook or ignore those concerns? How does God want to use us to bring people to repentance?

Anger or Applause?

How do we react when God shows mercy to people we think deserve punishment? If we are resentful, it may indicate that we have forgotten how much the Lord has forgiven us.

After Jonah followed God's second call to preach His coming judgment on Nineveh (Jonah 3:1–4), the people of the city turned from their evil lifestyle, so the Lord did not destroy them (v. 10). God's mercy made Jonah angry. He told God he had been afraid this would happen, and that's why he fled to Tarshish in the first place. "I know that You are a gracious and merciful God, . . . One who relents from doing harm" (4:2).

But the Lord said to Jonah, "Should I not pity Nineveh, that great city, in which are more than one hundred and twenty thousand persons?" (4:11).

God's marvelous grace is greater than all our sin. "For by grace you have been saved through faith, and that not of yourselves; it is the gift of God" (Ephesians 2:8). Because of His grace to us, we should "be kind to one another, tenderhearted, forgiving one another, even as God in Christ forgave [us]" (4:32).

Instead of being angry when God is merciful, we should applaud.

—David McCasland

JONAH 3:10—

Then God saw their works, that they turned from their evil way; and God relented.

■ Read today's
Our Daily Bread at
www.rbc.org/odb

5

The Rest of the Story

WHAT HAPPENED NEXT? How does this story end? Don't we always want to know "the rest of the story"?

It may be that Jonah finally came to understand the need for mercy to overwhelm judgment. If this weren't true, why else would he write about his own experience and finish it in God's words about the value He places on eternal souls?

In the month or so it would have taken Jonah to travel back to Gath

Hepher, God's rebuke probably weighed heavily on his heart.

Imagine him traveling alone on the return journey with all of those events relating to this excursion running through his mind.

The subsequent conviction could have become so strong that by the time he returned home, he had a heart of love and compassion for the lost—even for those who were his enemies.

Maybe Jonah even realized that when our enemies come to faith in God, they're not our enemies anymore. Aren't you thankful that Jonah wrote his story with frankness and honesty so we could be reminded why love is always better than hate?

Failure Versus Success

We learn many lessons in the book of Jonah, but the thread that connects them all together is the mercy of God. We see it in His pursuit and restoration of Jonah, His sparing of the sailors, and His miraculous salvation of Nineveh. Also in full view is the spiritual failure of Jonah . . .

- who experienced mercy but gave none;
- who received love but returned none;
- who benefited from the patience of God but resented God for showing that same patience to Nineveh.

■ FOCAL POINT

"Jonah and his self-pity fade away, and the Jonahs among the listening circle feel that Yahweh is putting the question to them personally. The story is deliberately left open-ended and the listeners are brought face to face with the existential challenge of the story."

—Leslie C. Adams
The New International Commentary on the Old Testament

"The final verses of the book clearly focus on God's right to destroy or to deliver. For Jonah the problem of God's forgiving Nineveh lies not so much in their wickedness, although this is obviously a related factor, but rather in the fact that they will be responsible for the destruction of Israel. How can God allow this to happen? This is the real dilemma confronting Jonah."

DESMOND ALEXANDER
Obadiah, Jonah and Micah

It's easy to forget that the one who is forgiven much should love much, and the one who has received mercy should be merciful.

There's an old hymn that says, "There's a wideness in God's mercy like the wideness of the sea." But even that's not wide enough. The ultimate expression of the wideness of God's mercy is that of the outstretched arms of Christ nailed to a cross and dying for our sins.

How each of us responds to that mercy is the issue on which our eternity hangs. Jonah was "successful" in running from God's mercy, but his greatest failure was in not wanting others to be allowed to experience that mercy. God grant that we would succeed in gratefully and obediently taking His mercy to those who need it as much as we do.

5 The Rest of the Story

STUDY GUIDE
read pages 51–53

To capture the final lessons of Jonah's stories.

MEMORY VERSE
Jonah 4:2—

"I know that you are a gracious and merciful God, slow to anger and abundant in lovingkindness, One who relents from doing harm."

Warming Up

When have you benefited from taking some time to think through what God has brought into your life? Often we respond immediately, but how has taking a little extra time helped you gain a better perspective?

Thinking Through

1. Bill Crowder observes that "love is always better than hate" (p. 52). While we all know that to be true philosophically, in what ways does the church find it difficult to let love overcome hate?

2. God's mercy shines through in the book of Jonah. It is what saved the disobedient Jonah from death and it rescued the Ninevites from sure destruction. Where have you seen God's mercy at work in your life or the life of others who are followers of Christ?

3. Jonah was responsible, as much as his prophecy helped relay God's message, for Nineveh's ability to continue on. But Jonah fears something, as the quote by Desmond Alexander on page 53 indicates. What worries Jonah?

Going Further

Refer

Jonah is referred to in other passages besides the book that bears his name: 2 Kings 14:25; Matthew 12:39-41; Matthew 16:4; and Luke 11:29–30. What significant facts come from those references?

Digging In

Read 2 Kings 14:25

1. Are you surprised to find Jonah in 2 Kings? What was Jonah's prophecy regarding Israel?

2. In the Jonah 4:2 passage, Jonah seems to fear God's mercy because of what it means in regard to Nineveh and Israel. If God had not been merciful to Nineveh, according to Jonah, how could that have protected Israel?

3. In Nahum 1, we can see the contrast between the light that Jonah brought and the later fate that would befall Nineveh when they rejected the God they had repented to earlier. What appears to be happening to Nineveh in this passage?

25 [Jeroboam] restored the territory of Israel from the entrance of Hamath to the Sea of Arabah, according to the word of the Lord God of Israel, which He had spoken through His servant Jonah the son of Amittai, the prophet who was from Gath Hepher.

Jonah 4:2

2 I know that you are a gracious and merciful God, slow to anger and abundant in lovingkindness, One who relents from doing harm.

Nahum 1:8–9

8 But with an overflowing flood He will make an utter end of its place, and darkness will pursue His enemies. 9 What do you conspire against the LORD? He will make an utter end of it. Affliction will not rise up a second time.

Prayer Time

Use the *Our Daily Bread* article on the next page as a guide for a devotional and meditation time relating to Jonah and success.

Reflect

What has the study of Jonah taught you about God's love, grace, and mercy?

What internal details in Scripture can lead us to see that Jonah is a true story, not an allegory or a parable?

Sign-Seekers

A skeptic once said to me, "I'll believe in Jesus if He comes down and appears visibly above my house." Not necessarily!

The Christ-rejecting religious leaders who requested a sign from Jesus had plenty of evidence for believing. They had undoubtedly heard of, if not seen, His miracles of healing, casting out demons, and even raising the dead. What more did they need?

Jesus therefore called them an "evil generation" (Luke 11:29). The only sign they would be given was the sign of Jonah the prophet, who had been thrown into a stormy sea (Jonah 1:2–3). When the Ninevites heard Jonah's message of repentance after he had spent three days in the belly of a fish, they believed God had sent him and they repented.

Likewise, the religious leaders who already knew of Jesus' words and works would soon see Him crucified and securely entombed. And in the following weeks they would hear personal testimonies from those who had seen Him alive, and had even touched Him, but they still wouldn't believe.

Today we have in the Gospels a record of what Jesus said and did, written by people who knew Him. If we are open to the truth, we have all the evidence we need to believe. We don't need to be sign-seekers.

—*Herb Vander Lugt*

Luke 11:29—
This is an evil generation. It seeks a sign, and no sign will be given to it except the sign of Jonah the prophet.

■ Read today's
Our Daily Bread at
www.rbc.org/odb

● LEADER'S and USER'S GUIDE

Overview of Lessons: Conquer Life's Challenges

Pulpit Sermon Series (for pastors and church leaders)

Although the Discovery Series Bible Study is primarily for personal and group study, pastors may want to use this material as the foundation for a series of messages on this important issue. The suggested topics and their corresponding texts from the Overview of Lessons above can be used as an outline for a sermon series.

DSBS User's Guide (for individuals and small groups)

Individuals—Personal Study
• Read the designated pages of the book.
• Carefully consider the study questions, and write out answers for each.

Small Groups—Bible-Study Discussion
• To maximize the value of the time spent together, each member should do the lesson work prior to the group meeting.
• Recommended discussion time: 45 minutes.
• Engage the group in a discussion of the questions—seeking full participation from each member.

Note To The Reader

The publisher invites you to share your response to the message of this book by writing Discovery House Publishers, P.O. Box 3566, Grand Rapids, MI 49501, USA. For information about other Discovery House books, music, videos, or DVDs, contact us at the same address or call 1–800–653–8333. Find us on the Internet at **dhp.org** or send e-mail to **books@dhp.org**.